Revised Edition

THE BOOK OF Playground Songs & Rhymes

Compiled by John M. Feierabend

GIA PUBLICATIONS, INC. * CHICAGO

Compiled by
John M. Feierabend

G-8747

GIA Publications, Inc.
7404 S. Mason Avenue
Chicago, IL 60638

Printed in the
United States of America.
ISBN: 978-1-62277-690-0

Table of Contents

Introduction

Here is a great collection of songs and rhymes that invite beat motions from students in the mid to late elementary grades.

Compiling this collection was truly a joy as many of the songs, rhymes and games I recalled from my own childhood playing on sidewalks or driveways. For many hours, especially in the summer, the neighborhood kids would gather to skip rope, bounce balls, play hand clapping games or choose one another to be the first "it" in a game with a counting-out rhyme. It is interesting to think that since there was no elementary music program in the schools where I grew up that the other kids were my first music teachers. I delighted in learning a new counting out rhyme, or being challenged with a jump rope chase game. In addition, my mother Alice knew dozens of these songs and rhymes and would enjoy sharing them with us kids. I can't chant "One, Two, Three, A-leary-o" and not see her lifting her leg over the ball, or clap "My Mamma Gave Me a Nickel" without hearing her voice singing it.

The songs and rhymes in this book, more than any other, were the roots of my own musical development, and the community we made playing these games no doubt inspired me years later to advocate building community through music.

Teachers should share these songs and rhymes with their students during music class and then leave a few playground balls and jump ropes in a box outside their classroom door. Let the students know they may borrow them at any time for recess or after school. Perhaps then, today's students will discover the same joy I did by sharing the songs, rhymes and games in this collection with their friends and family.

Hand Clapping

Introduction

Hand clapping rhymes were mostly played by pairs of children. Occasionally (as in "Four White Horses") two pairs join to form a group of four. Others (as in "Doctor Knickerbocker") organize the children into a standing circle and have them alternate clapping their own hands and then simultaneously clapping the hands of those on each side.

Here are a few basic hand-clapping patterns for a pair of children.

Pattern 1

Tap thighs
Clap own hands together
Clap partner's right hand
Clap own hands together
Clap partner's left hand
Clap own hands together
Clap both hands to both hands of partner
Clap own hands together

Pattern 2

Tap thighs
Clap own hands together
Clap partner's right hand
rest for one beat.
Tap thighs
Clap own hands together
Clap partner's left hand
rest for one beat.
Tap thighs
Clap own hands together
Clap partner's right hand
Clap own hands together
Clap partner's left hand
Clap own hands together
Clap both hands to both hands of partner
rest for one beat.

Pattern 3

Cross hands over chest
Tap thighs
Clap own hands together
Clap partner's right hand
Clap own hands together
Clap partner's left hand
Clap own hands together
Clap both hands to both hands of partner

A Sailor Went To Sea

Additional Verses

Verse 2

A sailor went to chop, chop, chop,
To see what he could chop, chop, chop,
And all that he could chop, chop, chop,
Was the bottom of the deep blue chop, chop, chop.

Verse 3

A sailor went to knee, knee, knee....

Verse 4

A sailor went to toe, toe, toe....

Verse 5

A sailor went to ooh-washy-wash....

Verse 6

A sailor went to sea, chop, knee, toe, ooh-washy-wash....

Directions

A	*clap own hands together*
sai -	*clap partner's right hand*
lor	*clap own hands together*
went	*clap partner's left hand*
to	*clap own hands together*
sea, sea, sea	*clap both hands to both hands of partner, three times (front back front)*

Repeat pattern until the end.

Direction Variation

Substitute the following motions in the clapping sequence instead of "front, back, front."

Each time on the words "sea, sea, sea"–salute three times.

Each time on the words "chop, chop, chop"–chop one hand onto the other hand three times.

Each time on the words "knee, knee, knee"–tap knees three times.

Each time on the words "toe, toe, toe"–tap on toes three times.

Each time on the words, "Ooh-washy-wash"–twist body back and forth like a washing machine.

Each time on the words, "see, chop, knee, toe, ooh-washy-wash"–perform only one of each of the designated motions in sequence.

Bobo Ski Aden

Directions

Two children face each other and perform the following hand clapping pattern:

1. *Clap both palms to both palms of partner*
2. *Tap back of your hands to back of partner's hands*
3. *Clap own hands together*
4. *Clap partner's right hand*
5. *Clap own hands together*
6. *Clap partner's left hand*
7. *Clap own hands together*
8. *Clap both palms to both palms of partner*

Four White Horses

Directions

Four people stand in a circle. Each person is across the circle from his/her partner. The eight-beat clapping pattern is as follows:

1. *Clap own hands together*
2. *Clap both hands to both hands of your corner. (Couple one turns to the person on their right; couple two turns to the person on their left)*
3. *Clap own hands together*
4. *Clap both hands with your other corner. (Couple one turns to the person on their left; couple two turns to the person on their right)*
5. *Clap own hands together*
6. *Clap both hands to both hands of partner (Couple one claps high, couple two claps under couple one's hands)*
7. *Clap own hands together*
8. *Clap both hands to both hands of partner (Couple one claps low, couple two claps over couple one's hands)*

Head and Shoulders Baby

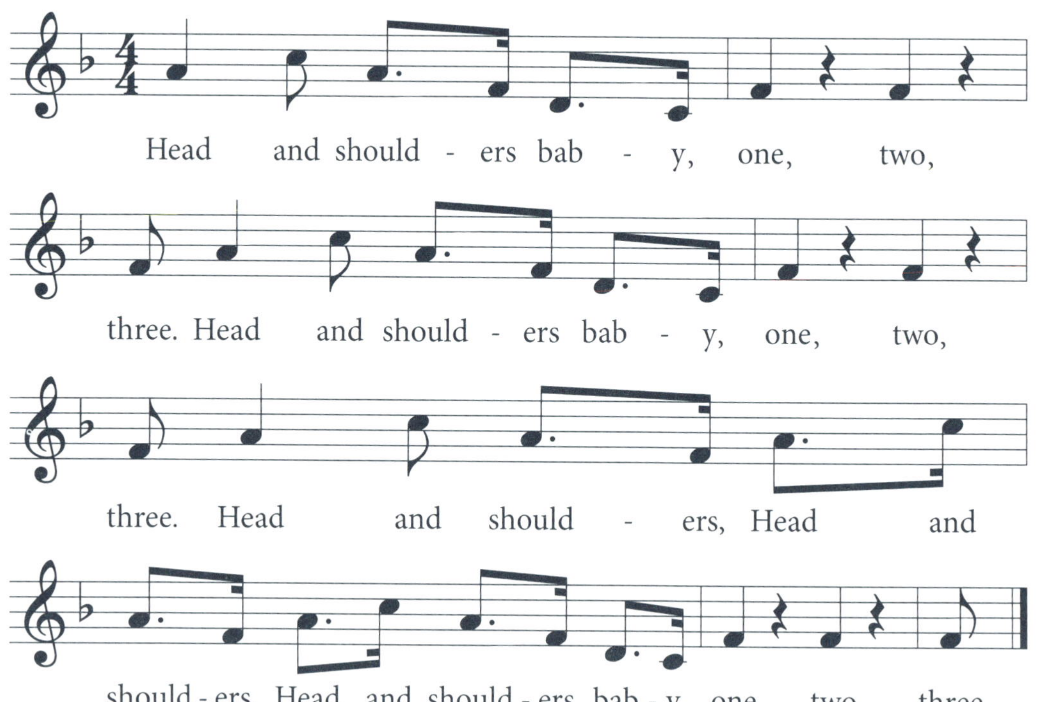

Additional Verses

Verse 2

Knees and ankles baby, one, two, three.
Knees and ankles baby, one, two, three.
Knees and ankles, Knees and ankles,
Knees and ankles baby, one, two, three.

Verse 3

Milk the cow baby....

Verse 4

Throw the ball baby...

Directions

Tap the body part as mentioned or pantomime the motion as in "milk the cow" or "throw the ball."

Head	*touch head*
shoulders	*touch shoulders*
baby one	*clap hands together*
(rest)	*clap partner's right hand*
two	*clap hands together*
(rest)	*clap partner's left hand*
three	*clap both hands to both hands of partner*

Hot Cross Buns

Directions

Hot *clap own hands together*
Cross *clap both hands to both hands of partner*
Buns *clap own hands together*
(rest) *tap both hands on own legs*
Hot *clap own hands together*
Cross *clap both hands to both hands of partner*
Buns *clap own hands together*
(rest) *tap both hands on own legs*

One a *clap own hands together*
penny *clap partner's right hand*
two a *clap own hands together*
penny *clap partner's left hand*
Hot *clap own hands together*
Cross *clap both hands to both hands of partner*
Buns *clap own hands together*
(rest) *tap both hands on own legs*

I Am a Pretty Little Dutch Girl

Additional Verses

Verse 2

My boyfriend's name is Fatty,
He comes from Senorati,
With turned-up toes and a pimple on his nose,
And that's the way the story goes.

Verse 3

First he gave me peaches,
Then he gave me pears,
And then he gave me twenty-five cents,
To kiss me on the stairs.

Verse 4

I gave him back his peaches,
I gave him back his pears,
I gave him back his twenty-five cents
And kicked him down the stairs.

Long Legged Sailor

Additional Verses

Verse 2

No I never, never, never, in my long legged life,
Saw a long legged sailor and his long legged wife.

Verse 3

Did you ever ... short legged....

Verse 4

No I never ... short legged....

Verses 5 and 6

...bow legged....

Verses 7 and 8

...one legged....

Verses 9 and 10

...no legged....

Directions

Did	*place both hands on legs*
you	*clap own hands together*
ever	*clap partner's right hand*
ever	*clap own hands together*
ever	*clap partner's left hand*
in your	*clap own hands together*
long	*spread own hands apart, indicating length*
legged	*clap own hands together*
life	*clap partner's right hand*
see a	*clap own hands together*
long	*spread own hands apart, indicating length*
legged	*clap own hands together*
sailor	*clap partner's left hand*
and his	*clap own hands together*
long	*spread own hands apart, indicating length*
legged	*clap own hands together*
wife	*place both hands on legs*

Additional Motions

(perform action only on the descriptive word)

long	*spread own hands apart, indicating length*
short	*spread own hands apart; shorter length*
bow	*stand with feet together and knees apart*
one	*lift one leg behind*
no	*rapidly lift both legs behind; a very quick jump*

Miss Lucy

Additional Verses

Verse 2

He drank up all the water, He ate up all the soap,
He tried to eat the bathtub, But it wouldn't go down his throat.

Verse 3

Miss Lucy called the doctor, Miss Lucy called the nurse,
Miss Lucy called the lady with the alligator purse.

Directions

The eight beat clapping pattern begins with "Miss":

1. *Clap both hands to both hands of partner*
2. *Tap back of your hands to back of partner's hands*
3. *Clap own hands together*
4. *Clap partner's right hand*
5. *Clap own hands together*
6. *Clap partner's left hand*
7. *Clap own hands together*
8. *Clap own hands together behind your back*

Miss Mary Mack

Additional Lyrics

All dressed in black, black, black
With silver buttons...
All down her back...
She asked her mother...
For fifty cents...
To see the elephant...
Jump over the fence...
He jumped so high...
He reached the sky...
And he didn't come back...
'Til the fourth of July...

Directions

Miss	*arms crossed on chest*
Ma-	*place both hands on legs*
ry	*clap own hands together*
Mack	*clap partner's right hand*
(rest)	*clap own hands together*
Mack	*clap partner's left hand*
(rest)	*clap own hands together*
Mack	*clap both hands to both hands of partner*

(continue clapping pattern from beginning)

Money Honey

My land - lord rang the front door bell,
I let it ring for a long, long spell, I
went to the win - dow, I peeked out the blind, I
asked that man what was on his mind. He said,
"Mon - ey hon - ey, Ooo - - - ee,
Mon - ey hon - ey, Ooo - - - ee, If you
wan - na get a - long with me, If you
wan - na get a - long with me."

Directions

1. *Clap own hands together*
2. *Clap partner's right hand*
3. *Clap own hands together*
4. *Clap partner's left hand*
5. *Clap own hands together*
6. *Clap both hands to both hands of partner*
7. *Arms crossed on chest*
8. *Tap thighs with both hands*

My Momma Gave Me a Nickle

Verse 2

My momma gave me a dime to buy a lime,
I didn't buy that lime, I bought some chewing gum.
Some chew, chew, chew, chew, chewing gum, some chew, chew, chewing gum,
I didn't buy that lime, I bought some chewing gum.

Verse 3

My momma gave me a quarter for soda water,
I didn't buy the water, I bought some chewing gum. Some chew....

Verse 4

Momma gave me a dollar, to buy a collar,
I didn't buy the collar, I bought some chewing gum. Some chew....

My Mommy Told Me

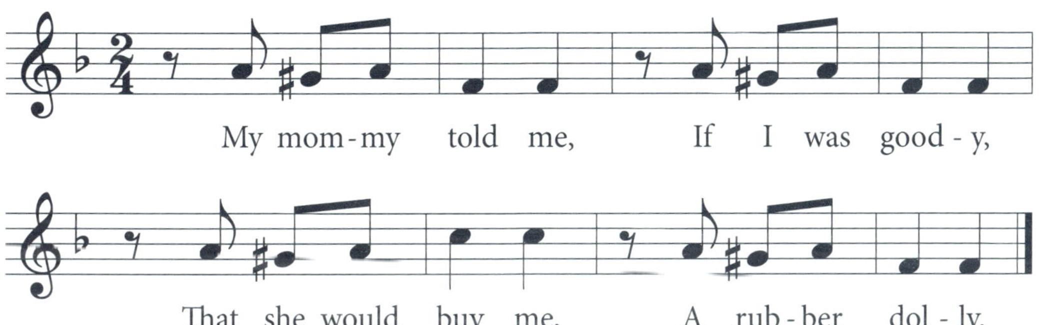

Verse 2

My auntie told her,
I kissed a soldier,
Now she won't buy me,
A rubber dolly.

Say, Say, My Playmate

Verse 2 (Optional)

Say, say, my playmate,
I cannot play with you,
My dolly has the flu,
boo, hoo, hoo, hoo, hoo, hoo.
Say, say, my playmate,
I cannot play with you.
But, we'll be jolly friends forever more.

Directions

Say	*arms crossed on chest*
say	*place both hands on legs*
my	*clap own hands together*
play	*tap legs twice*
mate	*clap own hands twice*
(rest)	*clap both hands to both hands of partner*
come	*tap back of your hands to back of partner's hands*
out	*clap both hands to both hands of partner*
and	*clap own hands together*

(continue clapping pattern from "playmate")

Stooping on a Window

Directions

Perform some hand clapping pattern with a partner throughout.

Pat-a-Cake

Pat-a-cake, pat-a-cake, baker's man.
Bake me a cake as fast as you can.
Roll it and pat it and mark it with a "B,"
And put it in the oven for baby and me.

Pease Porridge Hot

Pease porridge hot.
Pease porridge cold.
Pease porridge in the pot,
Nine day old.
Some like it hot.
Some like it cold.
Some like it in the pot,
Nine days old.
My mammy likes it hot.
My pappy likes it cold.
But, I like it in the pot,
Nine days old.

Three, Six, Nine

Three, six, nine,
The goose drank wine.
The monkey chewed tobacco,
On the street car line.
The line broke.
The monkey got choked.
They all went to heaven,
In a little rowboat.

Clapping in a circle

Doctor Knickerbocker

Doc-tor...

Rapidly pat legs alternating hands. Then alternate clapping own hands with hands of person on each side.

Knickerbocker, Knickerbocker,
Number nine.

You can keep a rhythm most any
old time.

Now let's put the rhythm in our
feet.

Stop clapping and stomp one foot and then the other, then continue the hand clapping pattern beginning with clapping own hands on "Now."

Now let's put the rhythm
on our legs.

Stop clapping and tap legs two times, then continue the hand clapping pattern beginning with clapping own hands on "Now."

Now let's put the rhythm
in our hands.

Clap hands two times and resume the hand clapping pattern beginning with clapping own hands on "Now."

Now let's put the rhythm
on our heads.

Stop clapping and tap head two times. Repeat the entire rhyme with motions several time, each time faster.

When Billy Boy Was One

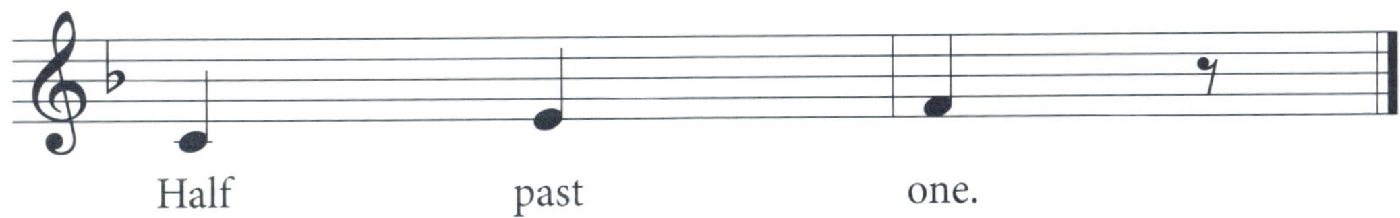

Additional Verses

Verse 2

When Billy Boy was two, two, two,
He learned to tie his shoe, shoe, shoe.
Oh, shoe me over, shoe me over,
Half past two.

Verse 3

...three...he learned to climb a tree....

Verse 4

...four...he learned to shut the door....

Verse 5

...five...he learned to do the jive....

Verse 6

...six...he learned to pick up sticks....

Verse 7

...seven...he almost went to heaven....

Verse 8

...eight...he learned to shut the gate....

Verse 9

...nine...he learned to climb a vine....

Verse 10

...ten...he learned to say "THE END!"....

Directions

When	*clap own hands together*
Bil-	*clap partner's right hand*
ly	*clap own hands together*
Boy	*clap partner's left hand*
was	*clap own hands together*
one	*clap both hands to both hands of partner*
one	*tap back of your hands to back of partner's hands*
one	*clap both hands to both hands of partner*
He....	*(continue from beginning)*
Half	*clap partner's right hand*
(rest)	*clap own hands together*
past	*clap partner's left hand*
(rest)	*clap own hands together*
one	*clap both hands to both hands of partner*
(rest)	*tap back of your hands to back of partner's hands*
	clap both hands to both hands of partner

Jump Rope

Introduction

Before 1900 jump rope was primarily a boy's competitive game with tricks and endurance challenges. Rhymes were not usually spoken. In the twentieth century, as people moved from rural areas to urban areas, and skirts became shorter, girls took up the game and added rhymes, sometimes from other known games such as ball bouncing or counting out rhymes. By the 1920s jump rope became almost completely a girls game.

While chanting the rhymes, a single person could jump rope twirling the rope by themselves, but jump rope was more often played with a pair of twirlers, one on each end, and a third person jumping in the middle. Jump roping shifted from being competitive boys game to being a game of cooperation.

Basic jumping involves two jumps for each rotation of the rope, a larger jump as the rope passes under and a smaller jump to fill the time before the next pass of the rope. Jumpers can jump with both feet, hop on the right, hop on the left or alternate hopping on the right and then the left. "Hot Pepper" rhymes invite the jumper to make single jumps for each pass.

"Jumping in" and "jumping out" of the twirling rope takes a bit of practice. Beginners might want to start with a stationary rope. The twirlers then begin to twirl the rope giving the jumper time to prepare for the first jump.

Competitive jump roping demonstrates multiple possibilities while jumping ropes. The jump rope songs and rhymes in this book are the ones mostly performed in playgrounds. In the following rhymes two children hold the ends and twirl a long jump rope while a third child jumps to the rhyme. If there are only two children, one end of the rope can be tied to something like a fence or a doorknob, and the twirler holds the other end.

Blue Bells Cockle Shells

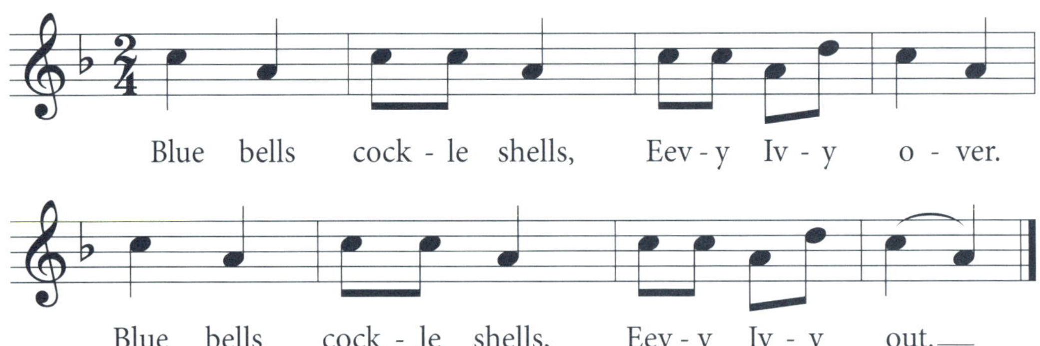

Directions

Two twirlers gently swing the rope back and forth while the one in the middle jumps. On the word "over" the twirlers begin twirling the rope while the one in the middle jumps. On the word "out" the jumper jumps out.

Rhymes for One Jumper

Don't Say Ain't

Don't say ain't,
Your mother will faint.
Your father will fall in a bucket of paint.
Your sister will cry,
Your brother will die.
The dog and the cat will say "Good-bye."

Fatty and Skinny

Fatty and Skinny went to bed,
Fatty rolled over and Skinny was dead.
Fatty called the Doctor and the Doctor said,
"That's what you get for rolling in bed."

Fudge, Fudge, Call the Judge

Fudge, Fudge, call the judge,
Mamma's gonna have a baby.
It isn't a girl, it isn't a boy,
It's just a new born baby.
Wrap it up in tissue paper, send it
down the elevator.
First floor skip.
Second floor skip.
Third floor don't skip,
Stop the rope by not jumping
Cause momma's gonna have a baby!

Hello, Hello, Hello, Sir

"Hello, hello, hello, sir,
Meet me at the grocer."
"No sir."
"Why sir?"
"Because I have a cold sir."
"Where'd you get your cold, sir?"
"At the North Pole, sir."
"What were you doing there, sir?"
"Shooting polar bear, sir."
"Let me hear you sneeze, sir."
"Kachoo, kachoo, kachoo, sir."

He Took Her to the Garden

He took her to the garden,
And set her on his knee.
And said, "Baby, please,
Will you marry me?"
Yes, no, maybe so, yes, no, maybe so.

I am a Pretty Little Dutch Girl

I am a pretty little Dutch girl,
As pretty as she can be,
And all the boys around the block,
They want to marry me.
My boy friend's name is Paddy,
He comes from Cincinnati,
With a cherry on his nose
and ten fat toes,
and that's the way my story goes.

I'd Rather Wash the Dishes

I'd rather wash the dishes,
I'd rather scrub the floor.
I'd rather kiss the garbage man,
Than kiss the boy *(girl)* next door.

I Had a Little Brother

I had a little brother, his name was Tiny Tim,
I put him in the bathtub to see if he could swim.
He drank up all the water, he ate up all the soap,
And out comes bubbles, when he jumps rope.

I Had a Little Chicken

I had a little chicken,
And he wouldn't lay an egg.
So I poured hot chocolate
Up and down his leg.
He wiggled and he jiggled,
And he stood on his head.
Funny little chickie,
Laid a hard boiled egg.

I Hate to Wash the Dishes

I hate to wash the dishes,
I hate to scrub the floor,
I'd rather kiss my sweetheart,
Behind the kitchen door.
How many kisses will I get?
1, 2, 3...etc....

I Know a Woman and Her Name is Miss

I know a woman and her name is Miss.
And all of a sudden she goes like this.
Jumper stops the rope.

Intry, Mintry, Cutry Corn

Intry, mintry, cutry corn,
Appleseed and apple thorn.
Wire, brier, limber, lock,
Twelve geese in a flock.
One flew east, and one flew west.
One flew over the cuckoo's nest.

I Saw a Birdie in the Sky

I saw a birdie in the sky,
It dropped some whitewash in my eye.
But, I'm a big boy, I don't cry.
I'm just glad that cows can't fly!

I See London, I See France

I see London, I see France.
I see *(someone's)* underpants!

I Went to the Pictures

I went to the pictures next Tuesday
And took a front seat at the back.
And said to the lady behind me,
I can't see over your hat.
She gave me some well-broken
cookies,
I ate them and gave her them back.
I fell from the pit to the balcony,
And broke my front bone at the back.

Jelly in the Bowl

Jelly in the bowl,
Jelly in the bowl,
Wiggy, waggy, wiggy, waggy,
Jelly in the bowl.

Lady Bug, Lady Bug

Lady bug, lady bug
Fly away home,
Your house is on fire,
And your children will burn.
Jump out

Late Last Night

Late last night and the night before,
Twenty-four robbers came knockin' at
my door.
I got up and let them in.
I knocked them on the head with a
rolling pin.

Matthew, Mark, Luke and John

Matthew, Mark, Luke and John
Went to bed with their trousers on.
Mark cried out in the middle of the
night,
"Oh, my trousers are too tight!"

Miss, Miss, Little Miss

Miss, Miss, Little Miss,
When she misses, she misses like this.
Jumper stops the rope.

My Momma Gave Me a Nickel

My momma gave me a nickel to buy a pickle.
I didn't buy a pickle, I bought some chewing gum.
My momma gave me a dime to buy a lime.
I didn't buy a lime, I bought some chewing gum.
My momma gave me a quarter, to buy some water.
I didn't buy the water, I bought some chewing gum.

Miss Monroe Broke Her Toe

Miss Monroe broke her toe,
Riding on a buffalo.
The buffalo died and Miss Monroe cried,
And that was the end of the buffalo ride.

Obediah Jumped in the Fire

Obediah jumped in the fire.
The fire was so hot, he jumped into a pot.
The pot was so little, he jumped into a kettle.
The kettle was so black, he jumped in a crack.
The crack was so high, he jumped to the sky.
The sky was so blue, he jumped in a canoe.
The canoe was so shallow, he jumped in the tallow.
The tallow was so hard, he jumped into the lard.
The lard was so soft, he jumped in the loft.
The loft was so rotten, he fell into the cotton.
The cotton was so white, he stayed all night.

Old Lady, Old Lady

Version 1

Old lady, old lady,
Lived in a shoe.

Version 2

Old lady, old lady,
What'll you do?
Old lady, old lady,
Stubbed her toe.
Old lady, old lady,
Out you go! *(jump out)*

Version 3

Old lady, old lady,
Touch the ground.
Old lady, old lady,
Turn around.
Old lady, old lady,
Point your shoe.
Old lady, old lady,
23 skidoo!
Jump out.

One Bright Day

One bright day in the middle of the night,
Two dead boys got up to fight.
Back to back they faced each other,
Drew out their swords and shot each other.
A deaf policeman heard the noise,
Came and shot the two dead boys.
If you don't believe this lie is true.
Ask the blind man, he saw it too.

One, Two, Three, Four, Five, Six, Seven

One, two, three, four, five, six, seven,
All good children go to heaven.
Seven, six, five, four, three, two, one,
All bad children suck their thumbs.

Ooey Gooey Was a Worm

Ooey gooey was a worm,
A little worm was he.
He sat upon the railroad tracks,
The train he did not see.
Ooey gooey!

Standing on the Corner

Standing on the corner, chewing bubble gum,
Along came a little boy, asked me for some.
"No, you little boy, No, you dirty bum,
Can't have any of my bubble gum."

Teacher, Teacher I Declare

Teacher, Teacher I declare,
I see *(someone's)* underwear!

There was a Little Fellow

There was a little fellow and his name was Jack,
He wanted to go to heaven in a Cadillac.
The carburator broke and down he fell,
Instead of going to heaven he went to....
Now don't you get excited, don't you lose your head,
Instead of going to heaven, he went to bed.

Tommy Tucker Went to France

Tommy Tucker went to France,
To teach the ladies how to dance.
First the heel and then the toe,
Turn around and out you go!
Jump out.

Two, Four, Six, Eight

Two, four, six, eight,
Meet me at the garden gate.
If I'm late, don't wait.
Two, four, six, eight.

Way Down South

Way down south where bananas grow,
A grasshopper stepped on an elephant's toe.
The elephant cried with tears in his eyes,
"Why don't you pick on someone your own size!"

La Reina

Additional Verses

Verse 2

Soy la reina de los mares,
ustedes lo van a ver,
tiro mi pañuelo al suelo
y lo vuelvo a recoger.

Verse 3

Si la cosa no se acaba,
la culpa la tienes tú,
por andar de parrandera
con tu vestidito azul.

Translation

I am the Queen of the seas,
you will see,
I throw my scarf to the floor
And I will pick it up.

If things do not end,
the fault is yours,
to go out on the town
with your blue dress.

How Far Can You Count?

Blondie and Dagwood

Blondie and Dagwood went to town,
Blondie bought an evening gown.
Dagwood bought a pair of shoes,
Cookie read the evening news.
This is what Cookie read.
This is what the paper said;
"Close your eyes and count to ten,
And if you miss you take an end."
1, 2, 3....

Close eyes and jump up to ten then jump out

Bread and Butter

Bread and butter
Sugar and spice.
How many boys,
Think I'm nice?
1, 2, 3...etc....

Bubble Gum, Bubble Gum

Bubble gum, bubble gum in a dish.
How many pieces do you wish?
1, 2, 3...etc....

Bumble Bee, Bumble Bee

Bumble bee, bumble bee, stung
Jack Fry.
How many feet did it make him fly?
1, 2, 3....

Cinderella Dressed in Yella

Cinderella dressed in yella
Went upstairs to kiss a fella.
Made a mistake and kissed a snake,
Came downstairs with a tummy ache.
How many doctors did it take?
1, 2, 3...etc....

Cinderella Thinks She's Cute

Cinderella thinks she's cute,
All she wears is a bathing suit.
If you can count to twenty two,
There's one more turn a-waitin' you.

Jump and count to 22. If you don't miss you get another turn!

Dennis the Menace

Dennis the Menace has a squirt gun.
He took it out and had some fun.
He shot a man in the foot.
How many squirts did he shoot?
1, 2, 3...etc....

Doctor, Doctor, Tell No Lie

Doctor, doctor, tell no lie,
How many years until I die?
1, 2, 3...etc....

Down in the Valley

Down in the valley where the green
grass grows,
There sat Helen, pretty as a rose.
She sang, she sang, she sang so sweet,
Along came Johnny and kissed her on
the cheek.
How many kisses did she receive?
1, 2, 3...etc....

Grace, Grace, Dressed in Lace

Grace, Grace, dressed in lace,
Went upstairs to powder her face.
How many boxes did she use?
1, 2, 3....

Granny, Granny I Am Ill

Granny, Granny I am ill,
Send for the doctor to get give me
a pill.
Doctor, doctor, shall I die?
Yes, you must and so must I.
How many carriages shall I have?
10, 20, 30....

Count until the jumper misses.

Here Comes the Teacher

Here comes the teacher with a big fat stick,
Now get ready for arithmetic.
1, 2, 3...etc....

I Eat My Peas with Honey

I eat my peas with honey.
I've done it all my life.
It makes them taste quite funny.
But it keeps them on my knife.
How many peas stick on my knife?
1, 2, 3...etc....

Jelly Fish, Jelly Fish

Jelly fish, jelly fish,
In a dish.
A wiggle, waggle, waggle,
And a two, four, six.
Not because you're dirty,
Not because you're clean,
Not because you kissed a boy,
Behind a magazine.
How many kisses did you receive?
1, 2, 3...etc....

Johnny Gave Me Apples

Johnny gave me apples,
Johnny gave me pears.
Johnny gave me fifty cents
And kissed me on the stairs.
I gave him back his apples,
I gave him back his pears.
I gave him back his fifty cents,
And kicked him down the stains.
How many stairs did he fall down?
1, 2, 3...etc....

Mickey Mouse

Mickey Mouse bought a house
Under an apple tree.
Mickey Mouse called his house
Number twenty-three.
1, 2, 3...etc....*(up to twenty three)*

My Mother Owns a Butcher Shop

My mother owns a butcher shop,
My father cuts the meat,
And I am just their little kid,
Who runs across the street.
How many times do I cross?
1, 2, 3...etc....

Peel an Orange

Version 1

Peel an orange, nice and round.
See if you can touch the ground.
If you can, do it again,
Close your eyes and count to ten.
1, 2, 3...*(up to ten then jump out)*

Version 2

Peel an orange, nice and round.
Peel a banana upside down.
If you can count to 24
You can have an extra turn!
1, 2, 3... *(up to 24)*

Sally Over the Water

Sally over the water,
Sally over the sea,
Sally broke a milk bottle
And blamed it on me.
I told Ma,
Ma told Pa,
Sally got a lickin'
Ha, ha, ha!
How many lickins did she receive?
1, 2, 3...etc....

Sugar, Salt, Pepper and Cider

Sugar, salt, pepper and cider,
How many legs on a bow-legged spider?
1, 2, 3...etc....

Teacher, Teacher, Oh, So Tired

Teacher, Teacher, oh, so tired,
How many times were you fired?
1, 2, 3...etc....

Oliver Twist

Directions

While the rope goes around once for each measure, perform motions as indicated.

Say the Alphabet

Ice Cream Soda

Ice cream soda, lemonade pop,
Tell me the 'nitials of your sweetheart.

Say the alphabet until there is a miss. Sometimes the twirlers gradually go faster to ensure a miss before the end of the alphabet.

Strawberry Shortcake

Strawberry Shortcake, cream on top.
Tell me the letter of your sweetheart.

Say the alphabet jumping out on the letter of your sweetheart.

Sweet and Sour Pickles

Sweet and sour pickles,
Sugar cake and cream.
Tell the initials of my dream.

Say the alphabet jumping out on the letter of your sweetheart.

Fast Rope Turns at the End

Fast rope turns at the end are called "hot peppers."

Johnny Over the Ocean

Johnny over the ocean,
Johnny over the sea,
Johnny broke a teacup,
And blamed it on me.
I told Ma,
Ma told Pa,
Johnny got a lickin'
Ha, ha, ha!
Salt, vinegar, mustard, pepper!
Twirl the rope very fast.

Mabel, Mabel

Mabel, Mabel,
Set the table.
Don't forget
The Red Hot Pepper!
Twirl the rope very fast and count by fives.

Motor Boat, Motor Boat

Motor boat, motor boat, go so slow.
Motor boat, motor boat, start to go.
Motor boat, motor boat, go so fast.
Motor boat, motor boat, step on the gas!
Twirl the rope very fast.

Old Man Daisy

Old man Daisy,
You're driving me crazy.
Up the ladder, down the ladder,
One, two, three.
Pepper, salt, vinegar
H-O-T!
Twirl the rope very fast.

One for the Money

One for the money,
Two for the show,
Three to get ready,
And four, let's go!
Twirl the rope very fast.

Policeman, Policeman

Policeman, policeman, do your duty,
Here comes *(someone)*, an American beauty.
She likes salt, but what she likes better,
Is plenty of that red hot pepper!
Twirl the rope very fast.

Postman, Postman

Postman, Postman, don't delay!
How many letters will come today?
Postman, Postman, pick up the pace.
Faster, faster. Lets have a race!
Twirl the rope very fast.

Robin Hood, Robin Hood,

Robin Hood, Robin Hood,
Dressed so good,
Got as many kisses
As he could.
How many kisses did he receive?
1, 2, 3...etc....
Twirl the rope very fast.

Strawberry Shortcake

Strawberry shortcake, cream on top,
Tell me the name of your sweet heart.
A, B, C, D....
What kind of a man will I marry?
Begin to twirl the rope faster and faster.
Rich man, poor man, beggar man thief,
Doctor, lawyer, Indian chief.

One In and Another Out

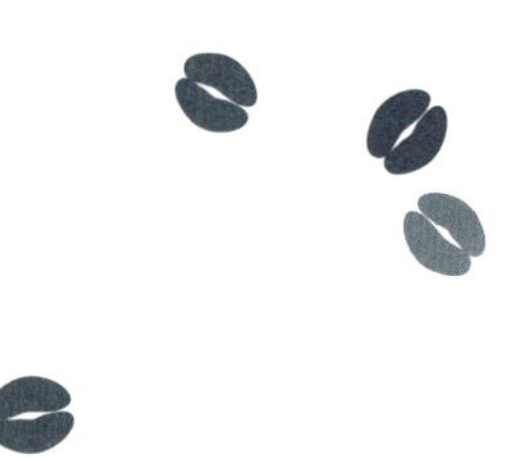

California Oranges

California oranges, fifty cents a pack.
Calling *(someone)* to tap me on the back.

"Someone" jumps in and taps the first jumper who then jumps out.

Down the Mississippi

Down the Mississippi,
Where the steamboats push.

A second jumper jumps in and pushes the first one out.

Icka Backa Soda Cracker

Icka backa soda cracker,
Icka Backa Boo.
Icka Backa soda cracker,
Out goes you.

A second jumper jumps in and pushes the first one out.

I Love Coffee, I Love Tea

I love coffee, I love tea,
I love ____________to jump with me.

Jumper (Child A) sings the name of another jumper to join him/her, at which time Child A jumps out and Child B repeats the rhyme supplying another child's name.

Jimmy and Robin Sittin' in a Tree

Jimmy and Robin sittin' in a tree,
K I S S I N G.
First comes love, then comes marriage,
Then comes ____________ in a baby carriage.

Jumper sings the name of the new person to jump in.

On a Mountain

Game

All sing the first four phrases while Child A jumps rope and two others twirl from the ends. Child A sings solo on, "Now, jump in_________" supplying another child's name. That child, Child B, then joins Child A, and sings, "Jump out__________," singing Child A's name, who then jumps out.

Miss Lucy Had a Baby

Miss Lucy had a baby,
His name was Tiny Tim.
She put him in a bathtub
To see if he could swim.
He drank up all the water.
He ate up all the soap.
He tried to eat the bathtub,
But it wouldn't go down his throat.
Miss Lucy called the doctor.
2nd child jumps in.
Miss Lucy called the nurse.
3rd child jumps in.
Miss Lucy called the lady
With the alligator purse.
4th child jumps in.
"Measles," said the doctor.
"Measles," said the nurse.
"Measles," said the lady
With the alligator purse.
Out goes the doctor.
2nd child jumps out.
Out goes the nurse.
3rd child jumps out.
Out goes the lady
With the alligator purse.
4th child jumps out.
And out goes ME!
1st child jumps out.

Polly Put the Kettle On

Polly put the kettle on,
And have a cup of tea.
In comes *(someone)*,
And out goes me.
The first jumper jumps out and the next jumper jumps in.

Rooms for Rent

Rooms for rent, inquire within.
When I move out let *(someone)* move in.
A second jumper jumps in as the first jumps out.

Sitting in the School Room

Sitting in the school room,
Chewing bubble gum.
In comes the principal,
And out goes the gum.
The first jumper jumps out and the next jumper jumps in.

This page intentionally blank.

Other Motions

Apple On a Stick

Apple on a stick,
Five cents a lick.
Every time I turn around
Turn around one time.
It makes me sick.

Grandma Moses Sick in Bed

Grandma Moses sick in bed,
Called for the doctor and this is what he said,
"Clap your hands, then slap the ground,
Do the Hokey Pokey, Then get out of town."

Hurry, Hurry Don't Be Late

Hurry, hurry don't be late.
Meet us at the garden gate.
Jump it high,
Jump it low.
Turn around and out you go!

I'm a Little Dutch Girl

I'm a little Dutch girl,
Dressed in blue.
These are the things I like to do.
Salute to the captain,
Salute.
Bow to the Queen,
Bow.
Turn my back,
Turn and face one of the twirlers.
On the Horse Marines.
I can do the wiggle,
Wiggle.
I can do the jig,
Jig
I can do the merry-go-round,
Turn around.
And I can do the split.
Jump out.

Marco Polo Went to France

Marco Polo went to France,
To teach the ladies how to dance.
Heel and toe and around you go.
Touch heel and toe and turn around.
Cross your legs and out you go.
Cross legs for one jump and jump out.

My Mother is a Dancer

My mother is a dancer,
Brother, can she twist.
She can do the Hoochie Coochie,
Just like this.
She can do the Can-Can,
She can do the splits,
She can do a tap dance,
Just like this.

Officer, Officer

Officer, Officer, do your duty.
Here comes *(someone)*, an American
beauty.
She can hobble, she can wobble,
She can even do the twist.
She can do most anything,
But she can't do this.
Jump on one foot, then on two.
Touch your toes, then run out the door.

One, Two, Buckle My Shoe

One, two, buckle my shoe.
Touch foot.
Three, four, shut the door.
Push hands out in front.
Five, six, pick up sticks.
Touch the ground.
Seven, eight, shut the gate.
Push hands out in front.
Nine, ten, do it again.
Jump out, and can jump back in to "do it again."

Oliver Twist

Oliver Twist, you can't do this,
So what's the use of trying?
Touch your heel.
Touch heel.
Touch your toe.
Touch toe.
Clap your hands,
Clap hands once.
And around you go.
Turn around.

Policeman, Policeman

Policeman, Policeman, do your duty,
Here comes *(someone)*, an American
beauty.
She can dance, She can sing.
She can do most anything.
But I bet ya ten dollars,
That she can't do this.
Turn around,
Touch the ground.
Get out of town.

Spanish Dancer

Spanish dancer, do the splits.
Kick legs out.
Spanish dancer, do high kicks.
Kick leg forward.
Spanish dancer, do the rounds.
Turn around.
Spanish dancer, touch the ground.
Touch the ground.
Spanish dancer, get out of town.
Jump out.

Teddy Bear, Teddy Bear

Teddy bear, teddy bear,
Turn around.
Turn around one time.
Teddy bear, teddy bear,
Touch the ground.
Touch the ground.
Teddy bear, teddy bear,
Show your shoe.
Jump on one foot.
Teddy bear, teddy bear,
Say "How do you do?"
Bow.
Teddy bear, teddy bear,
Go upstairs.
Lift knees to chest while jumping.
Teddy bear, teddy bear,
Say your prayers.
Hold hands like praying.
Teddy bear, teddy bear,
Turn out the light.
With one hand pull down the light cord.
Teddy bear, teddy bear,
Say, "Good night."
Jump out.

More Jumpers

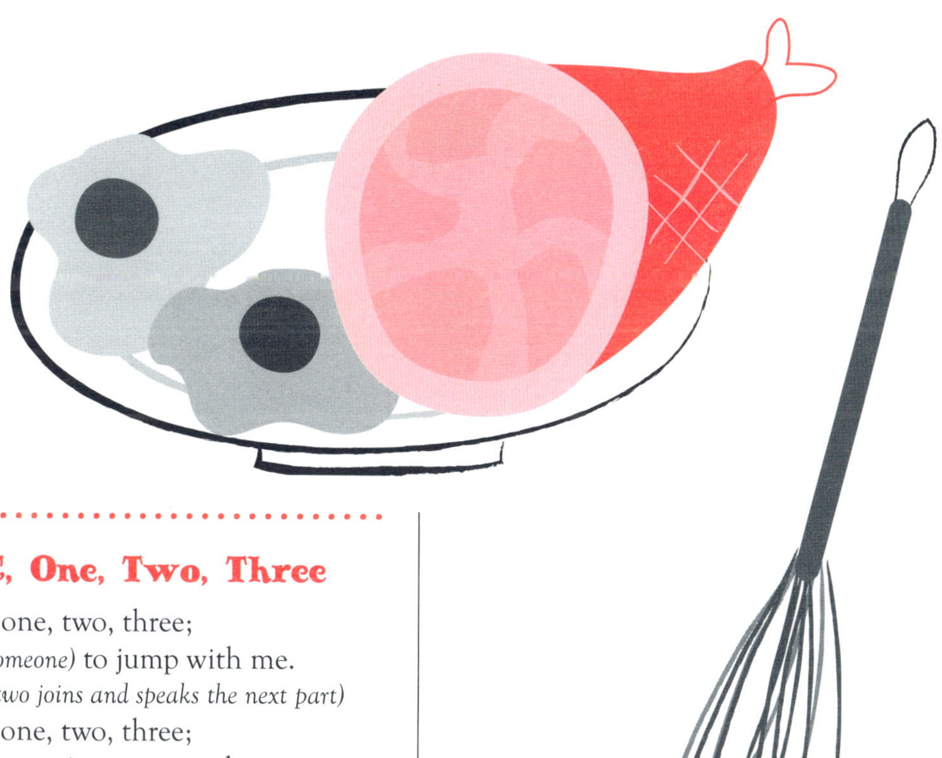

A, B, C, One, Two, Three

A, B, C, one, two, three;
I want *(someone)* to jump with me.
Jumper two joins and speaks the next part)
A, B, C, one, two, three;
I want *(someone)* to jump with me.
Jumper three joins and speaks the next part.
A, B, C, one, two, three;
I want *(someone)* to jump with me.
Continue for as many jumpers as you wish.

All in Together Girls

All in together girls, just like the weather girls.
When is your birthday?
Please jump in.
January.
February.
March. Etc....
When is you birthday?
Please jump out.
January.
February.
March. Etc....

Ham and Eggs

Start with one jumper.
Ham and eggs! Ham and eggs!
I like mine fried nice and brown.
Second jumper joins.
Ham and eggs! Ham and eggs!
Flip mine over, upside down.
Third jumper joins.
Ham and eggs! Ham and eggs!
Beat my eggs with a beater!
Scramble 'em, scramble 'em, scramble em!
Twirlers turn rope faster and faster.

Ball Bouncing

Introduction

Unlike the community intention of jump rope games, most ball bounces were done by one person at a time and then the ball was passed on to the next person. Many jump rope rhymes were also used for ball bouncing.

The two basic bouncing techniques were the "bounce-catch" and the "dribble-bounce." With the "bounce-catch" the ball is bounced on beats one and three and caught and held on beats two and four. The "dribble-bounce" requires the player to push the ball down on each beat. Many rhymes also required the player to coordinate bouncing the ball under a leg as the leg was lifted over the ball.

A Me-See, A Clap-See

Directions

Instead of bouncing the ball, the ball is tossed up in the air on each beat. In between the toss and catch various actions take place.

Me - see	*toss and catch*
Clap - see	*toss, clap hands and catch*
Twirl	*toss, twirl hands around each other and catch*
Bap-see	*toss, touch shoulders and catch*
Right hand	*toss with right hand and catch with both hands*
Left hand	*toss with left hand and catch with both hands*
High as the sky	*toss higher and catch*
Low as the sea	*bend forward and toss and catch*
Touch my knee	*toss, touch knee and catch*
Touch my toe	*toss, touch toe and catch*
Clap my hands	*toss, clap hands and catch*
Under we go	*bounce the ball and lift leg over the bouncing ball and catch the ball*

'Bounce High, Bounce Low

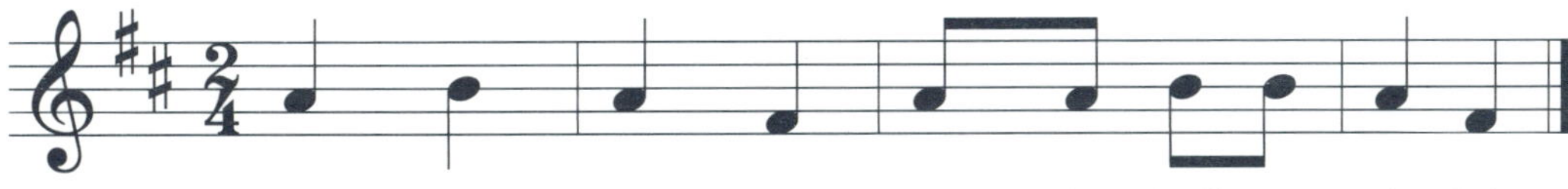

Directions

Children stand in a circle. One child bounces the ball on the beat then pushes the ball to some other child on the word "Shiloh"

One, Two, Three, Aleerie

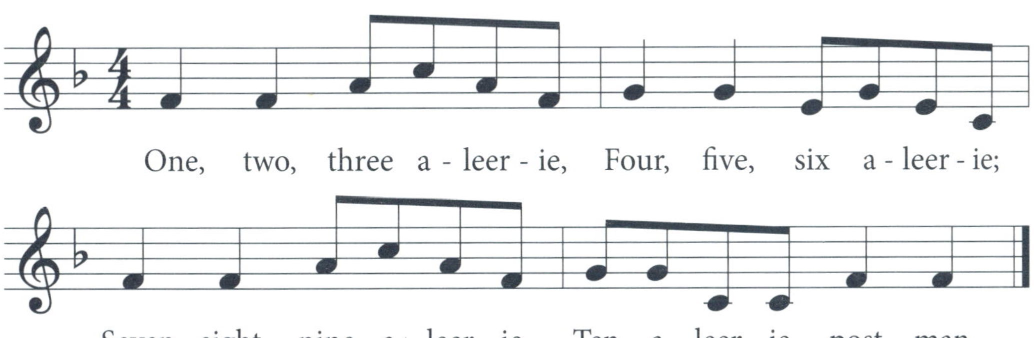

Directions

The ball is bounced on the beat. On the third beat, lift a leg over the ball as it is bounced.

A, My Name is Alice

A, my name is Alice
And my husband's name is Arnold.
We live in Alabama
And we sell apples.
B, my name is......

Continue with each letter of the alphabet.

Bouncy, Bouncy, Ball-y

Bouncy, bouncy, ball-y,
I lost the leg of my dolly.
My mommy came out and gave me a clout,
And turned my petticoat inside out.

Bounce the ball four times for each line. Lift leg over the ball on the last word.

Down the Mississippi

Down the Mississippi where the steam
boats go,
Some go fast and some go slow.
Down the Mississippi where the steam
boats PUSH!

The group stands in a circle. One person bounces the ball. On the final word the ball is bounced toward someone else.

One, Two, Three Aleerie-o

Directions

The ball is bounced five times for each line (four times on the last line). Each time "aleerie" is sung, lift a leg over the ball as it is bounced.

One, Two, Three O'Leary

Additional Verses

Verse 2

One, two, three O'Leary, I saw little Mary,
Sitting on a basketery, eating jelly beans.

Verse 3

One, two, three O'Leary, I saw little Mary,
Sitting on a missionary eating lady fingers.

Verse 4

One, two, three O'Leary, I saw little Mary,
Sitting in a cemetery eating plastic flowers.

Verse 5

One, two, three O'Leary, Mary's ball is down the alley,
Don't forget to give it to Mary, not to Charlie Chaplin.

Directions

The ball is bounced four times for each line. On the third beat, lift a leg over the ball as it is bounced.

Hello, Hello, Bill

Bounce the ball three times for each line.

Hello, hello, Bill,
Where are you going, Bill?
Uptown Bill.
What for, Bill?
To pay the gas bill.
How much, Bill?
A ten dollar bill.

Right Hand Beats a Booming Drum

Right hand beats a booming drum.
Bounce with the right hand.
Left hand beats a pan.
Bounce with the left hand.
But I can bounce my ball-o,
Bounce alternating hands.
Using either hand.

Hello, Hello, Hello, Sir

In the following rhyme the ball is bounced four times for each line. On the third beat, lift a leg over the ball as it is bounced.

"Hello, hello, hello, sir.
Meet me at the butcher."
"No, sir." "Why, sir?"
"Because I have a cold, sir."
Where'd you get the cold, sir?"
"At the North Pole, sir."
"What were you doing there, sir?"
"Counting polar bears, sir."
"How many did you count, sir?"
"One, sir; two, sir; three, sir; four, sir;
Five, sir; six, sir; seven, sir; eight, sir;
Nine, sir; ten, sir."
"Good-by, good-bye, good-bye, sir!
See you next July, sir."

Counting Out

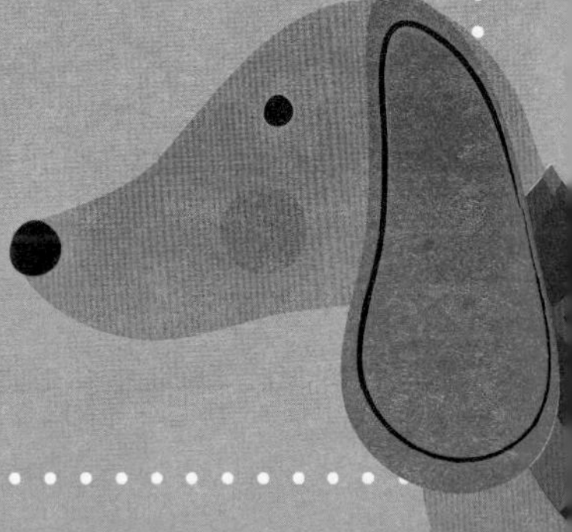

Introduction

Counting out rhymes (or choosing rhymes) are used to pick the next person to start a game, be the first to jump rope, or to determine who will twirl the jump rope. Children stand in a circle and each one puts a foot into the circle. One person chants the rhyme and touches each toe on the beat. Or, as an alternative, he might just point to each person or touch each person's chest as he goes around the circle.

Often the rhyme is only spoken one time to choose one person. Other counting out rhymes are repeated many times eliminating one person on each repetition until there is only one person left.

Many jump rope rhymes that end in counting can also be used as counting out rhymes. In these cases the rhyme is chanted while the pointer taps the beat on each person. The person being pointed to on the last word gets to chose a number from 1 to 10. Then the pointer taps one person per number. The last person pointed to is chosen.

The pointer can sometimes control who is or is not chosen by starting the counting on his own foot, or starting on the person next to him. Or, the pointer can add a tag to the end of the rhyme to add more beats such as "And out goes you" or "O-U-T spells out" or "My mother told me to choose the very best one."

All Around the Buttercup

All around the buttercup,
One, two, three.
If you want a partner
Just choose me.

Ana, Mana, Mona, Mike

Ana, mana, mona, Mike,
Barcelona, bona, strike.
Hare, ware, frown, wack
Halico, balico, wee, wo, wack!

As I Climbed Up the Apple Tree

As I climbed up the apple tree,
All the apples fell on me.
Someone shook them, and I knew,
The one who did was Y-O-U!

Big Bit, Little Bit

Big bit, little bit,
Have a fit, and you are it!

Bubble Gum

Bubble gum, bubble gum,
In a dish.
How many pieces,
Do you wish?
(child picks a number)
1, 2, 3...etc...and you are out.

Doggy, Doggy Diamond

Doggy, doggy diamond,
Step right out.
Not because you're dirty,
Not because you're clean,
Just because you kissed the girl
Behind the magazine.

Engine, Engine Number Nine

Engine, engine number nine,
Running down Chicago line.
If the train falls off the track,
Do I get my money back?
Yes, no, maybe so.
(Child says "yes" or "no.")
Y-E-S spells yes and you are out.

Ibbety, Bibbety, Gibbety, Goat

Ibbety, bibbety, gibbety, goat,
Ibbety, bibbity, bobbety, boat.
Dictionary, down the ferry,
Out goes YOU!

Icka, Backa, Soda Cracker

Icka, backa, soda cracker,
Icka, backa, boo.
Icka, backa, soda cracker,
I choose YOU!
(or "Out goes you")

Ickle, Ockle, Blue Bottle

Ickle, ockle, blue bottle,
Fishes in the sea.
If you want a pretty one,
Please choose me.

I Know Something

I know something I won't tell,
Three little rabbits in a peanut shell.
One can sing and one can dance,
One can make a pair of pants.
O-U-T spells out goes she!

Inka, Binka, Bottle of Ink

Inka, binka, bottle of ink
Cork fell out and you stink.
My mother told me to
Pick the very best one,
And that is Y-O-U!

Inky, Binky, Bonky

Inky, binky, bonky,
Daddy had a donkey.
Donkey died, Daddy cried,
Inky, binky, bonky.

Intery, Mintery, Cutery, Corn

Intery, mintery, cutery, corn,
Apple seed and apple thorn,
Wire, brier, limber lock,
Twelve geese in a flock,
One flew east and one flew west,
One flew over the cuckoo's nest.

Look Up

Look up, sky blue.
All out but YOU!

Mickey Mouse

Mickey Mouse, bought a house.
Couldn't pay the rent and got
kicked out!

My Mother, Your Mother

This is also used as a jump rope rhyme

My mother and your mother were
hanging up the clothes.
My mother punched your mother right
in the nose.
What color was the blood?
(child states "red" or "blue")
R-E-D spells red.
(or B-L-U-E spells blue)

One Potato, Two Potato

One potato, two potato,
three potato, four,
Five potato, six potato,
seven potato, more.

Each child stands with two clenched fists facing the center of the circle. The leader taps on each fist. At the end of the rhyme the last fist tapped is placed behind that persons back. The last fist left is the new "it."

**A variation of the above is to have all children sit in a circle with both legs out in front. The leader touches each foot. At the end of the rhyme the last foot touched is tucked under. The last leg still out is the winner.*

Onery, Twoery, Tickery, Seven

Onery, twoery, tickery, seven,
Alibi, crackaby, ten and eleven.
Pin, pan, muskadan,
Tweedle-dum, twoddle-dum,
Twenty-wan.
Eerie, ourie, owrie,
Out goes YOU!

Three Potatoes in a Pot

Three potatoes in a pot,
Take one out and leave it hot.

Two, Four, Six, Eight

Two, four, six, eight
Johnny caught a rattlesnake.
The snake he died, Johnny cried,
Two, four, six, eight.

Passing and Stick Games

Introduction

Passing Games are performed all over the world. Here are just a few examples.

Children sit close in a circle with their legs crossed so that their knees are almost touching those on either side. When first learning these games it is helpful to practice the beat motions of passing without using any objects (stones, sticks, cups). Once the passing motion is secure, try using only one object while all practice the passing motion. Finally, play the passing game starting with an object in front of every person.

Stick games can be played with rhythm sticks or Hawaiian puili sticks (which make a lovely sound when tapped).

Hakasot

Hebrew

Directions

Sit in a circle with legs crossed. Each person has a cup faced down in front of them.

Each picks up the cup on the upbeat and on the downbeat sets it down in front of the person to their right. Continue passing the cups to the right picking up the cup on beats 2 and 4 and setting the cups down on beats 1 and 3.

During the last measure, set the cup down in front of the person to the right on beat 1, but do not let go and bring the cup back and set it down in front of themselves on beat 2, and then set the cup down in front of the person to their right on beat 3.

Repeat many times. Sometimes when the game is played the tempo gradually increases.

I Pass the Shoe

Directions

Children sit in a circle with legs crossed and knees almost touching the knees of those on each side. With the right hand, have children tap the beat on the floor, first in front of themselves and then in front of the person to the right, while chanting, "In front, to the right, in front, to the right...." Once this motion is secure, have the group continue the tapping motion while a shoe (or some other object) is passed around on the beat. When the object lands in front of a child, his/her hand should land on it with the words, "In front" and he/she should then pass it to the right with the words, "to the right". Once passing on the beat is comfortable, try singing the song while the tapping and passing continues.

With advanced groups, try passing as many objects as there are children so all children are passing objects simultaneously through the song.

Makulai

Directions

Children sit in pairs facing each other. Each holds a pair of puili sticks. Use each pattern for an entire verse. Have children create new patterns.

3/4 beat patterns:

1. *Floor, tap together twice*
2. *Floor, with right hand tap left arm twice*
3. *Floor, with left hand tap right arm twice*
4. *Floor, with both hands tap left shoulder twice*
5. *Floor, with both hands tap right shoulder twice*
6. *Floor, with both hands tap left shoulder then right shoulder*
7. *Floor, cross arms and tap shoulders twice*
8. *Floor, tap both shoulders, cross arms and tap shoulders*

Obwisana

Directions

Children sit on the floor in a circle with their legs crossed so their knees are almost touching each other. Each child has a small object in front of him/her. With their right hand each child picks up the object and sets it down in front of the person on the right. The object should be set down at the beginning of each measure.

Nani Wale

Na - ni wa - le na ha - la, E - a, e - a.

O Na - u - e i - ke ka - i, E - a, e - a.

Ke on - i a e - la E - a, e - a.

Pi - li ma - i Ha e - na, E - a, e - a.

Directions

Puili Stick pattern: (8 beats each)

Repeat each pattern throughout or change pattern every 8 beats.

1. *Tap sticks together once - tap both on the floor three times (2 times).*
2. *Tap sticks together overhead - tap right stick on right shoulder,*
   Tap sticks together overhead - tap sticks on left shoulder (2 times).
3. *Tap sticks together overhead, leaning to the left (4 times) and to the right (4 times).*
4. *Tap sticks together overhead - tap right stick on right shoulder,*
   Tap sticks together overhead - tap sticks on left shoulder (2 times).

Other 8 beat patterns:

1. *Tap sticks together - tap sticks on floor (4 times).*
2. *Tap left shoulder with right stick - tap the floor with both sticks,*
   Tap the right shoulder with the left stick - tap the floor with both sticks (2 times).
3. *Tap sticks together - tap on the floor (4 times).*

Other 8 beat patterns facing partners:

1. *Tap sticks together - Tap right stick to partner's right.*
   Tap sticks together tap left to partner's left (2 times).
2. *Tap sticks on floor - toss right stick to partner - tap sticks on floor two more times (2 times).*
3. *Tap sticks on floor - toss left stick to partner - tap sticks on floor two more times (2 times).*
4. *Tap sticks on floor - toss both sticks to partner*

The Wonder Ball

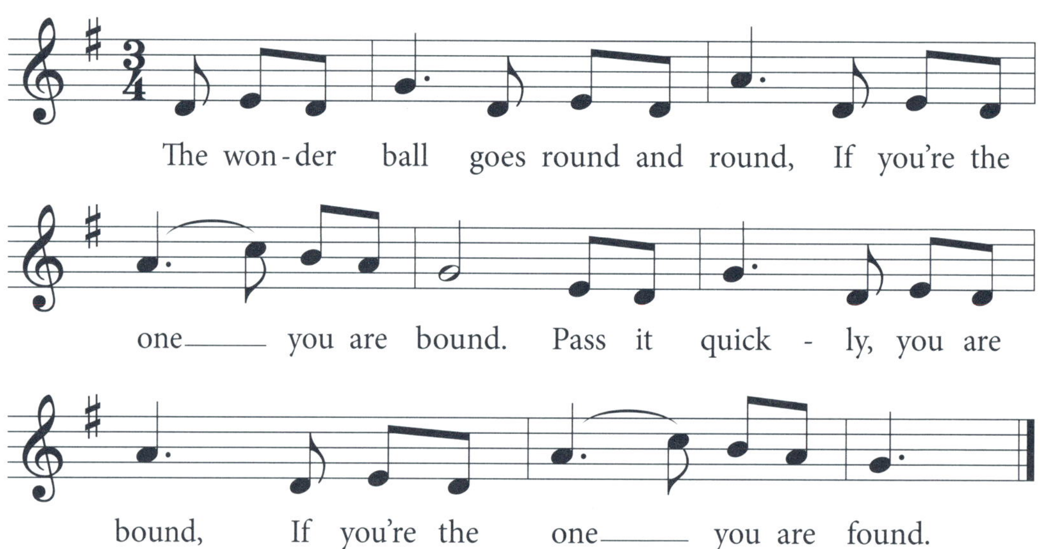

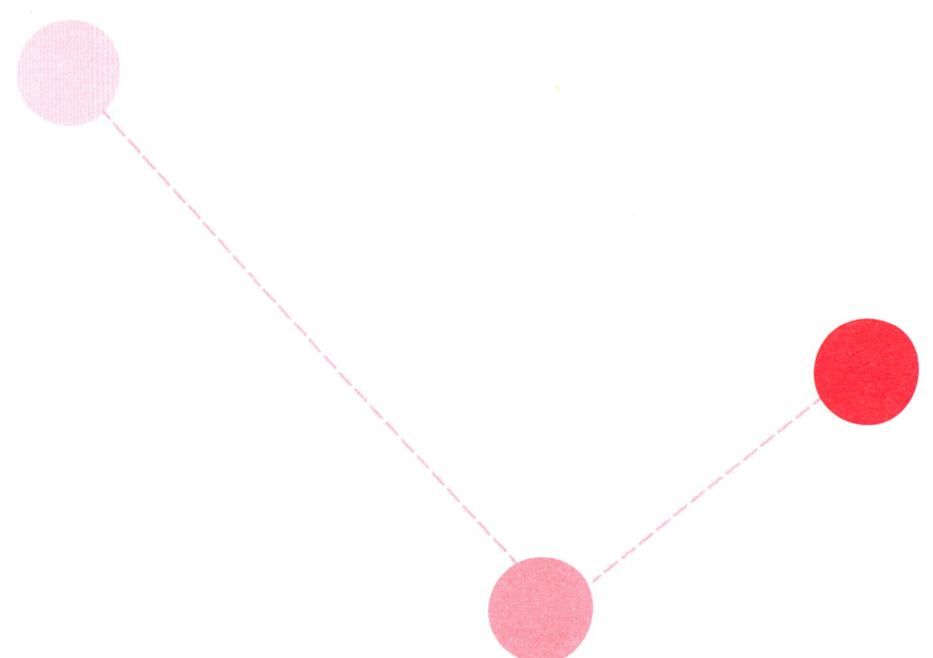

Directions

Pass a ball around a circle on the beat of the song.
The person receiving the ball on the last word "found" is out.
Continue repeating the game until only one person is left.

Where, Oh, Where

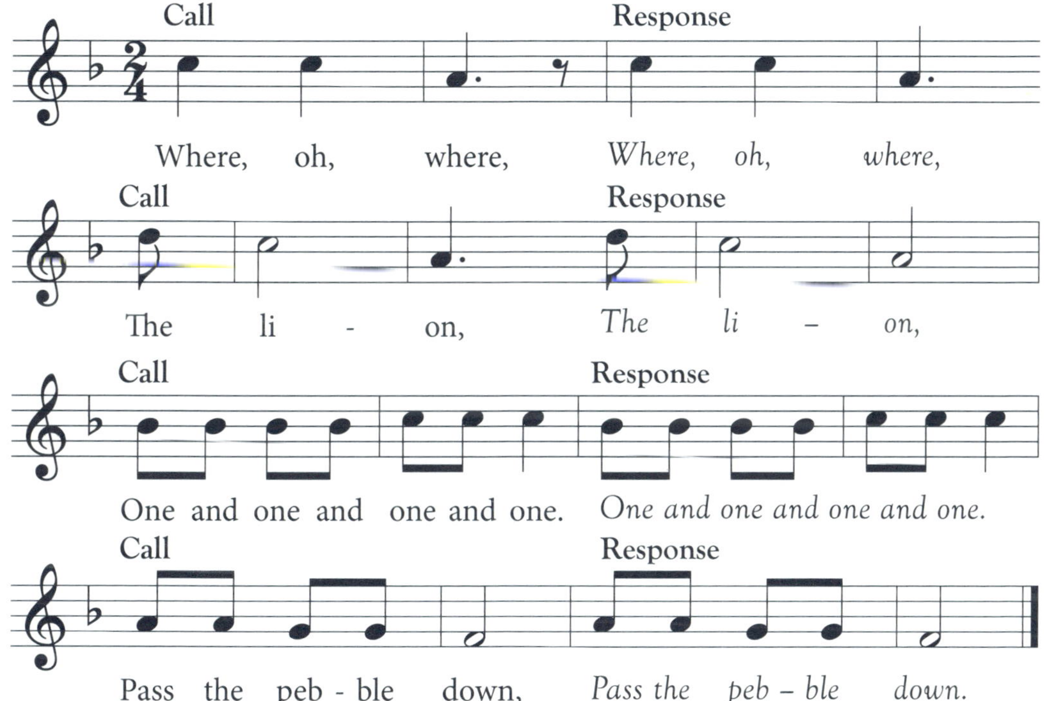

Directions

Children sit in a circle with their legs crossed and their knees almost touching.
Each child has a pebble in front of him/her.
The three motions should be practiced ahead of time.

1. *Pick up the pebble with the right hand.*
2. *Pass the pebble from the right hand to the left hand.*
3. *Set the pebble down in front of the person sitting to the left.*

This three-beat motion is especially fun with the two beat meter of the song.

Indexes

Songs/Rhymes by Title

Songs/Rhymes by Chapter by Title

Hand Clapping

Jump Rope

Ball Bouncing

Counting Out

Passing and Stick Games